My first words

SAN SERIF PRINT PROMOTIONS LIMITED
SERIF HOUSE, HADLEIGH ROAD, IPSWICH, SUFFOLK, IP2 0EE

This book belongs to:

- *Sherlock Holmes*
- Laurel & **Hardy**
- Joan of Arc
- Count Dracula
- _____ Write your own name in here _____
- ALB=RT EINSTEIN
- *Florence Nightingale*
- *William Shakespeare*

Art Director	Stefan Morris
Design	Millions Design
Illustration	Roma Bishop
Educational Consultant	Anne Hardy
Editor	Sheila Snow

Printed in Great Britain by BPCC Hazell Books, Paulton and Aylesbury

(Insert two 1·5v size AAA batteries)

Speaker

Lights

Questron®

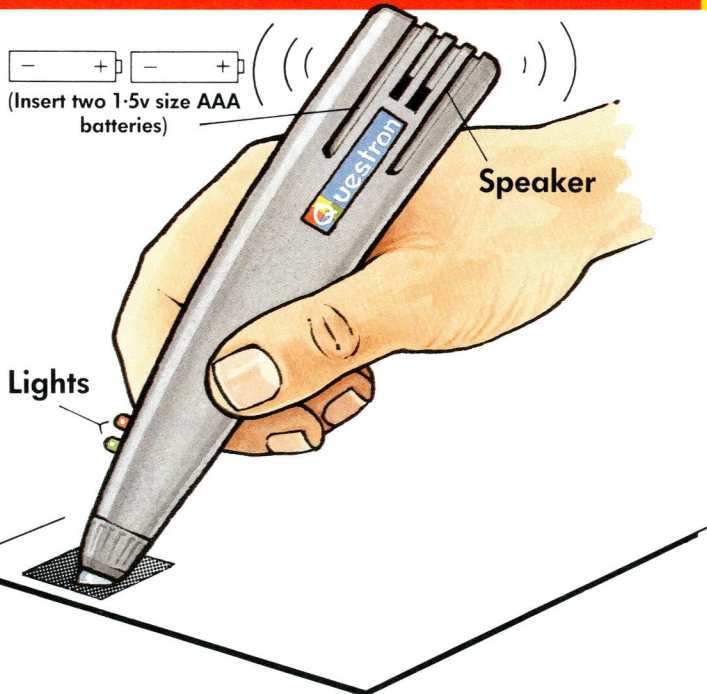

THE FUN WAY TO LEARN

INSTRUCTIONS

Press your pen on the answer squares. See the lights. Hear the sounds. (Press on the hats, too!)

Good

Try again

Well done!

Following a path, or 'tracking'

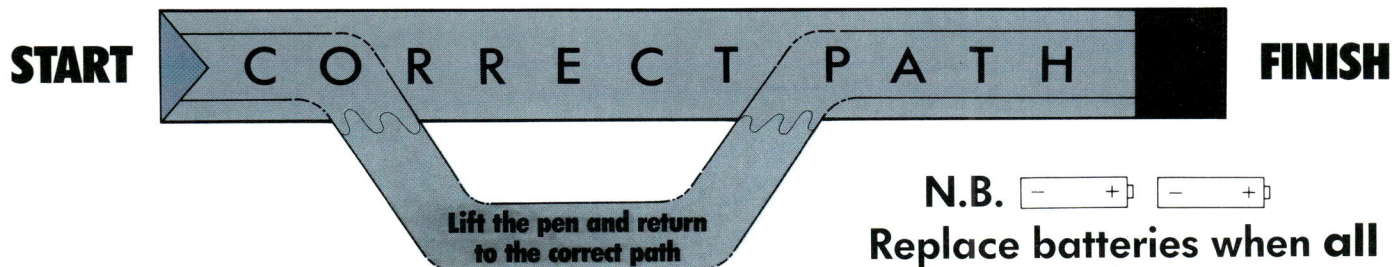

START **CORRECT PATH** FINISH

Lift the pen and return to the correct path

N.B. Replace batteries when **all** answers are given as correct.

A day out

Where shall we go today?
Trace over the path with Questron to find out.
Listen carefully.

Start here

farm

pond

park

shop

seaside

Listening is one of the early learning skills to be encouraged.

Ready to go

What do you think Bob and Rags need to take for a day at the seaside? Press the correct word boxes.

net

brush

bucket

bicycle

picnic

drum

towel

mop

boat

spade

ball

bed

flowers

swim suit

Questron helps a child to find the right answers.

First and last

Look at each pair of pictures.
Press Questron on the square in the picture that comes **first**.

Press Questron on the square in the picture that comes **last**.

Beach

9

On the farm

Bob and Rags the dog have a rest on the way. They see animals in a field. Press Questron on the name of the baby animal that belongs to each mother.

sheep

lamb

puppy

foal

cow

piglet

calf

kitten

pig

foal

duckling

piglet

dog

puppy

kitten

foal

duck

lamb

kid

duckling

cat

kitten

calf

piglet

horse

lamb

foal

calf

goat

kid

duckling

puppy

This matching game helps your child learn the correct names for baby animals.

Time for a break

Bob has to fix the car. Press Questron on the things that belong to a car.

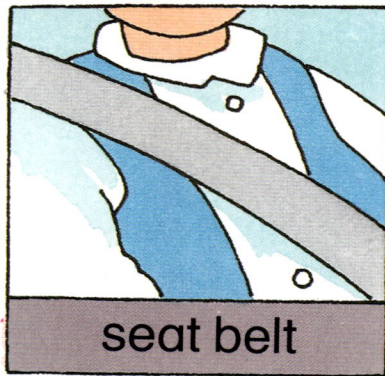

tyre

wheel

lamp

seat belt

boot

tools

chair

bonnet

map

light

umbrella

It is time for a picnic. Use Questron to choose what Bob and Rags will eat.

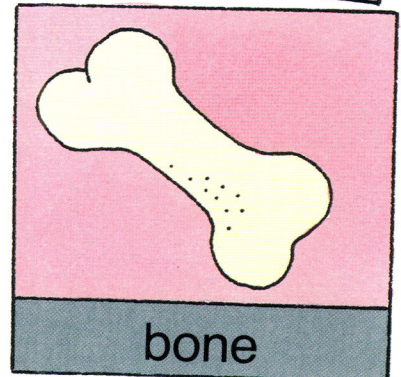

cup

bread

cheese

plate

banana

fork

apple

egg

milk

cake

bone

Ship ahoy!

Bob can see the sea. Use Questron to choose the correct word that tells about each object in the picture.

over

under

under

over

off

on

in front of

behind

off

on

behind

in front of

14

near

far

down

up

up

down

bottom

top

sit

stand

These are some of the words that your child will need to recognise when beginning to read.

15

At the seaside

The two friends are on the beach. Press Questron on the correct words that tell about the people and objects.

big

small

asleep

awake

wet

dry

happy

sad

loud

quiet

happy

sad

Look carefully at this page.
Then turn over and see what you can remember.

This page and the next are a memory game. Ask your child to tell you what is happening in the picture.

Now what can you remember?
Press Questron on the right answers.

Was the boy doing this?

Did you see a crab?

yes no

yes no

What was the girl holding?

Now turn back again and press Questron on these things.

ball

boat

bucket

18

Which are the same?

Look at the first thing in each row.
Press Questron on the thing in each row that matches it.

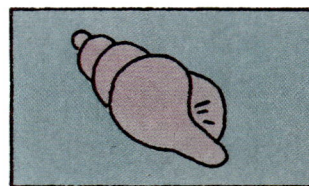

net	not	net	pet

boat	boat	boot	bone

ball	bull	bill	ball

Looking for matching objects and words is a useful early reading activity.

Getting dressed

Help Bob dress after his swim. Track Questron on the path that shows the piece of clothing Bob is going to put on next.

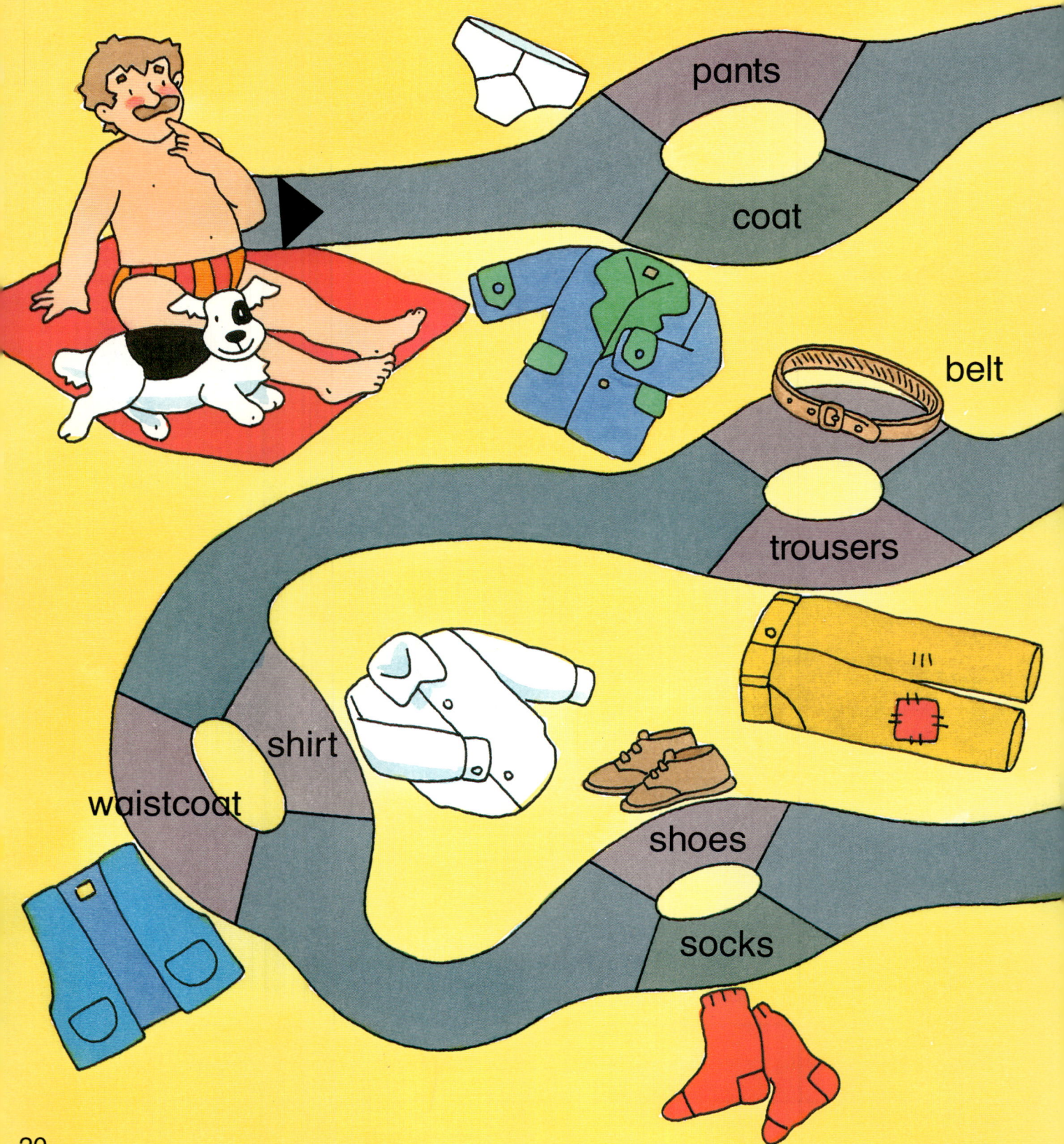

pants

coat

belt

trousers

shirt

waistcoat

shoes

socks

vest

waistcoat

socks

hat

belt

shirt

hat

vest

trousers

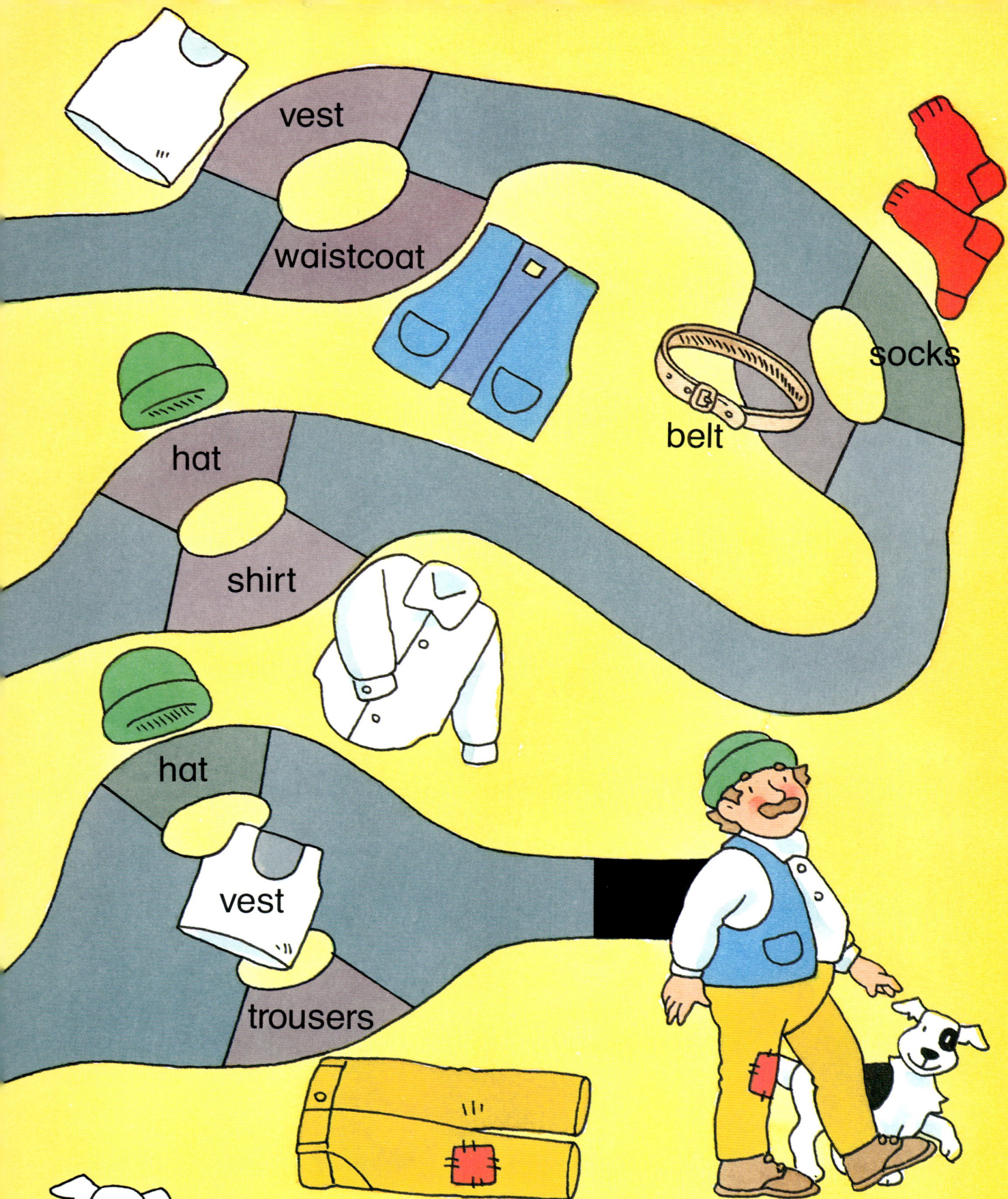

This is a visual discrimination and sequencing game.

Sail away

Use Questron to choose the correct number word that matches the numeral on each boat.

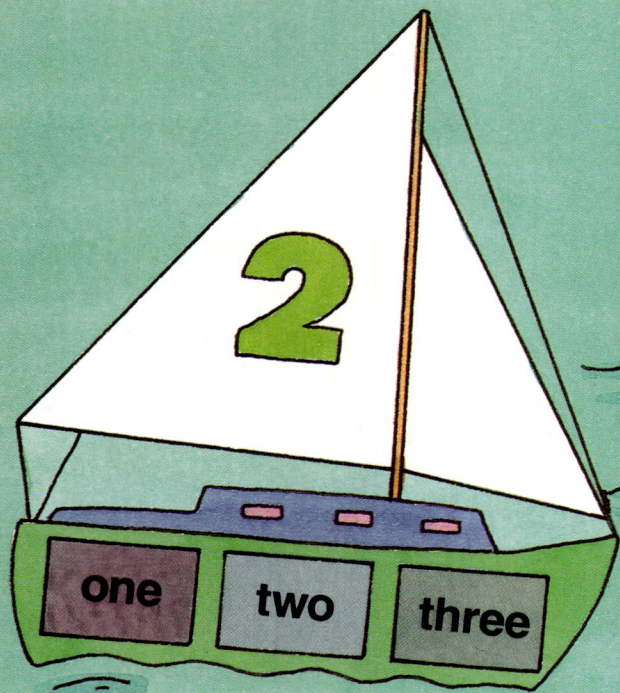

2

| one | two | three |

1

| seven | six | one |

3

| four | three | five |

5

| four | five | one |

6

six | nine | seven

4

two | four | eight

8

three | two | eight

9

three | six | nine

7

seven | one | ten

10

two | ten | three

Children need to be able to recognise the words for numbers.

23

Fishing

Press Questron on the colour word that matches the colour of each umbrella.

black

brown

yellow

green

blue

yellow

green

red

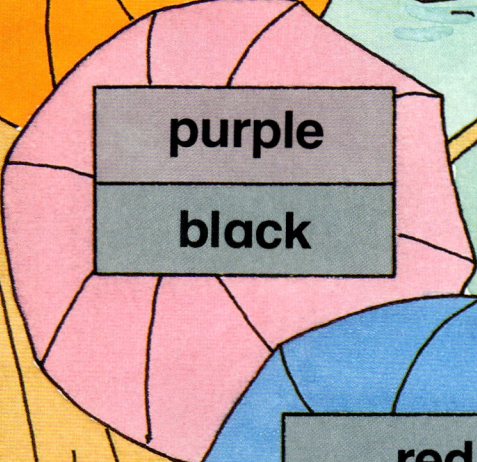

purple

orange

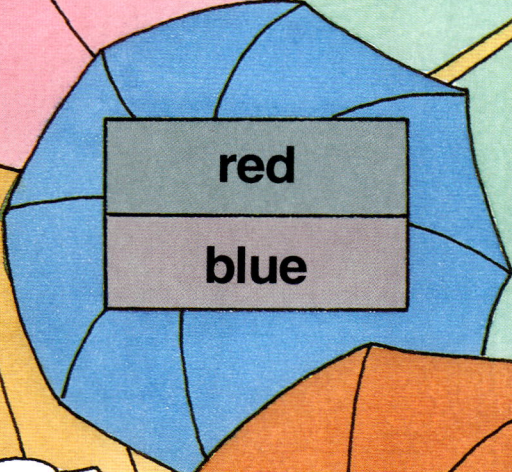

purple

black

red

blue

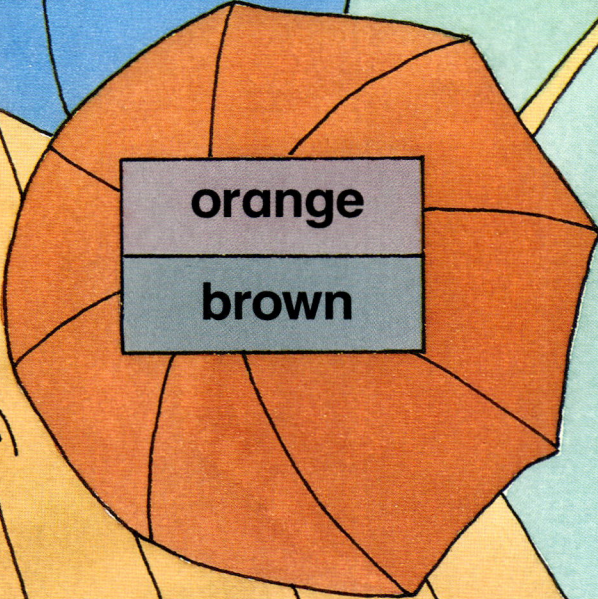

orange

brown

Fun at the fair

Press Questron on the correct answer to each question.

Which car is on your **left?**

Which mirror is in the **middle?**
Press the shirt.

Which child is on your **right?**
Press the shirt.

Which child is in the **middle?**

Who is at the **bottom?**

Which boy is at the **top?**
Press his hat.

These are some of the positional words your child will need to understand when beginning to read.

Story time

Look at the small pictures. With Questron, choose the sentence that tells about each picture.

Bob is in the car.

Bob is in bed.

Bob is at home.

The car is blue.

The car is red.

The boat is red.

Bob sees some ducks.

Bob sees a horse.

Bob sees some lambs.

Rags swims in the sea.

Rags runs fast.

Rags walks on the road.

The sun is in the sky.

The sun is behind a cloud.

The sun is blue.

The boat flies in the sky.

The boat goes on the road.

The boat sails on the water.

The sandcastle is in the sea.

The sandcastle is on the sand.

The sandcastle is green.

Bob is behind the car.

Bob is in front of the car.

Bob is beneath the car.

Questron helps a child find the right sentence.

Time to go

Help Bob and Rags find their way to the car.
Take Questron along the right route.

Start here ▶

Go in **front** of the ice cream man.

Go **around** the house.

Go in **front** of the duck pond.

Go **through** the trees.

Go **behind** the rabbits.

Take the **middle** path.

These are some of the phrases that your child will need to understand in the early stages of reading.

Questron®

THE FUN WAY TO LEARN

SAN SERIF PRINT PROMOTIONS LIMITED

SERIF HOUSE, HADLEIGH ROAD, IPSWICH, SUFFOLK, IP2 0EE